"The world fascinates me."

–Andy Warhol